Hillary Rodham Clinton

by
Sarah Tieck

South Huntington Pub. Lib.
145 Pidgeon Hill Rd.
Huntington Sta., N.Y. 11746

VISIT US AT
www.abdopublishing.com

Published by ABDO Publishing Company, 8000 West 78th Street, Edina, Minnesota 55439.

Copyright © 2010 by Abdo Consulting Group, Inc. International copyrights reserved in all countries. No part of this book may be reproduced in any form without written permission from the publisher. Buddy Books™ is a trademark and logo of ABDO Publishing Company.

Printed in the United States of America, North Mankato, Minnesota
092009
012010

Coordinating Series Editor: Rochelle Baltzer
Contributing Editors: Heidi M.D. Elston, Megan M. Gunderson, BreAnn Rumsch, Marcia Zappa
Graphic Design: Jane Halbert
Cover Photograph: *U.S. Department of State*
Interior Photographs/Illustrations: *AP Photo*: Elise Amendola (p. 26), AP Photo (p. 11), J. Scott Applewhite (pp. 5, 18), Alex Brandon (p. 29), Donald R. Broyles (p. 15), Lawrence Jackson (p. 28), Christina Jamison/NBC NewsWire via AP Photo (p. 25), Bill Pugliano (p. 21), Ed Reinke (p. 17), Reed Saxon (p. 19), Barry Thumma (p. 13), Susan Walsh, File (p. 23); *Getty Images*: Lee Balterman/Time Life Pictures (p. 9), Tim Boyle (p. 7), Steve Kagan/Time Life Pictures (p. 6).

Library of Congress Cataloging-in-Publication Data

Tieck, Sarah, 1976-
  Hillary Rodham Clinton / Sarah Tieck.
    p. cm. -- (First biographies)
  ISBN 978-1-60453-983-7
  1. Clinton, Hillary Rodham--Juvenile literature. 2. Presidents' spouses--United States--Biography--Juvenile literature. 3. Women legislators--United States--Biography--Juvenile literature. 4. United States. Congress. Senate--Biography--Juvenile literature. 5. Women presidential candidates--United States--Biography--Juvenile literature. 6. Women cabinet officers--United States--Biography--Juvenile literature. I. Title.
  E887.C55T54 2010
  973.929092--dc22
  [B]
                                                     2009031061

Table of Contents

Who Is Hillary Rodham Clinton? 4

Hillary's Family 6

Interest in Politics 8

A New Life 12

Family and Work 14

First Lady 16

Facing Challenges 20

Running for Office 22

Running for President 24

A New Dream 28

Important Dates 30

Important Words 31

Web Sites 31

Index 32

Who Is Hillary Rodham Clinton?

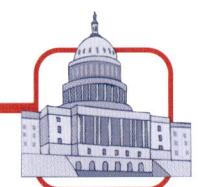

Hillary Rodham Clinton is a famous **politician** and author. She has helped shape U.S. laws and people's ideas.

Hillary has served her country in many ways. She has been the First Lady, a U.S. senator, and the secretary of state. Hillary has even run for president!

Few women in U.S. history have done these things. Hillary's work has helped create new opportunities for women.

Hillary often talks to news reporters about her work.

Hillary's Family

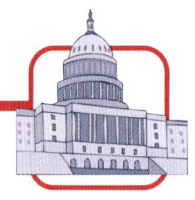

Hillary Diane Rodham was born on October 26, 1947. She was born in Chicago, Illinois.

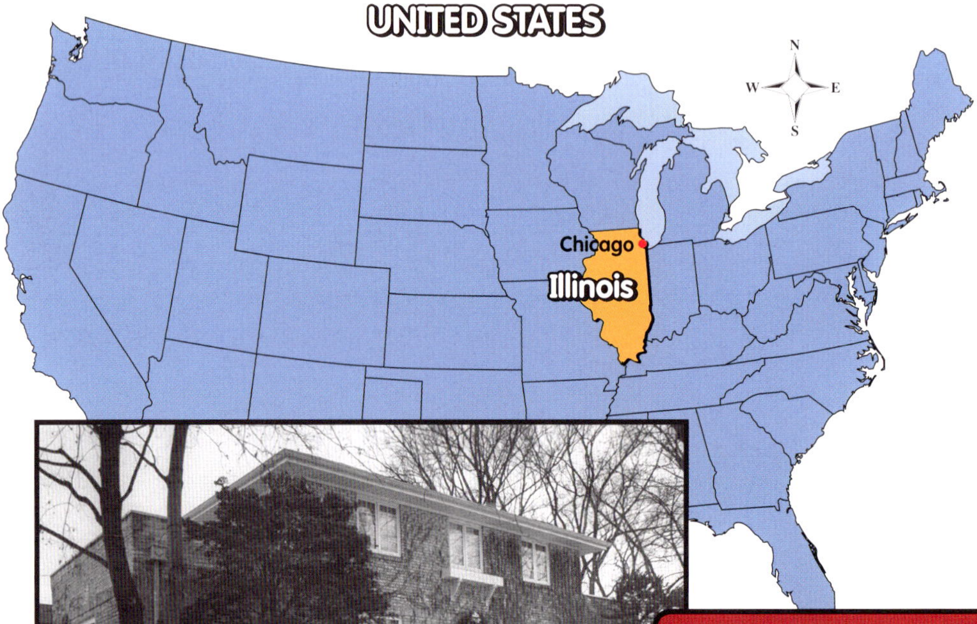

Hillary's family lived near Chicago in Park Ridge, Illinois.

During Hillary's childhood, women had fewer opportunities than they do today.

Hillary's parents are Hugh and Dorothy Rodham. Hillary has two younger brothers named Hugh and Tony.

Growing up, Hillary was a hard worker. She was smart and earned good grades in school. Hillary's parents told her to follow her interests.

Interest in Politics

In high school, Hillary discovered she enjoyed **politics**. Soon after, she began attending Wellesley College in Wellesley, Massachusetts. There, she studied politics. She even became president of the student government.

At her 1969 **graduation**, Hillary gave a speech. Many Americans heard about it and Hillary's ideas. Soon, her picture was in magazines and newspapers!

At Wellesley, Hillary had become interested in the **Democratic** Party. She wanted to learn more about **public service**. So, she attended Yale Law School in New Haven, Connecticut. She studied there from 1969 to 1973.

Hillary wanted to use her knowledge to help others.

After law school, Hillary began to work as a **lawyer**. She wanted to make a difference. So, she took a job working on children's rights in Massachusetts.

In 1974, Hillary began working on a **political** case. President Richard Nixon was having some troubles in office. Hillary helped **research** his **impeachment** case. Soon after, President Nixon left office.

President Nixon was the only president to give up his job.

A New Life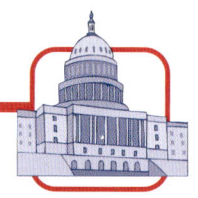

At Yale, Hillary had met a law student named Bill Clinton. Bill moved to Arkansas after **graduation**. In 1974, Hillary moved there to be near him. They married in 1975.

Hillary and Bill made their home in Little Rock, Arkansas. About a year later, Hillary started working at Rose Law Firm. Her life changed in 1978, when Bill was elected governor of Arkansas.

Hillary and Bill (*left*) shared a dream of reaching the White House.

Family and Work

Hillary and Bill became parents in 1980. Their daughter, Chelsea, was born on February 27.

This was a busy time for Hillary. As the governor's wife, she worked on many projects. She also became a top **lawyer** at Rose Law Firm.

Meanwhile, she and Bill wanted to help their country even more. So in 1992, Bill ran for president of the United States.

Hillary and Bill named their daughter for a famous song called "Chelsea Morning."

First Lady

In November 1992, Bill was elected president! In 1993, Bill, Hillary, and Chelsea moved into the White House in Washington, D.C.

As the president's wife, Hillary became the First Lady. She had her own office near the president's. No other First Lady had done this.

Some people thought Hillary was too bold. Others liked her hard work and fresh ideas.

Bill became U.S. president on January 20, 1993.

On the night Bill became president, he and Hillary attended several balls.

One part of the First Lady's job is to be the White House hostess. Hillary welcomed many visitors.

Hillary was First Lady for eight years. Like the president, the First Lady does important work.

Many First Ladies work on projects that are meaningful to them. Hillary worked to improve health care. And, she wanted to help children have better lives.

While First Lady, Hillary wrote a book called *It Takes a Village*. It is about her ideas for helping children.

Facing Challenges

When the Clintons moved to Washington, D.C., Chelsea was just 12. Hillary and Bill wanted her to have a normal childhood. A president's life can be very public. So, they did their best to keep Chelsea's life private.

Hillary and Bill also had some troubles while Bill was in office. In 1998, Bill was **impeached**. He continued working as president. But, this changed the way many people viewed Hillary and Bill.

Around 2003, Hillary wrote a book called *Living History*. It is about her life in the White House.

Running for Office

Bill would finish his term as president in 2001. Hillary wanted to continue serving her country. So, she decided to run for the U.S. Senate in New York.

In 2000, Hillary won the election! She was the first First Lady to run for a national office and win.

In 2001, Hillary became a U.S. senator. Senators work in Congress to help make important laws.

Hillary worked hard to make life better for people in New York and throughout the country. She was elected again in 2006.

As New York's senator, Hillary spent many days working at the U.S. Capitol.

Running for President

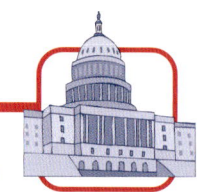

People all over the world noticed Hillary. They admired her hard work and success in office. Some thought she could become the U.S. president!

In 2007, Hillary announced that she would run for president. She hoped to become the first woman president of the United States.

Hillary spent much time campaigning to be the **Democratic candidate**. One of her main **rivals** was Barack Obama, a U.S. senator from Illinois.

During her campaign, Hillary traveled around the United States and gave speeches. Bill and Chelsea sometimes joined her.

Hillary wanted to help the Democratic Party win. So, she supported Barack as the Democratic candidate.

After many months, Barack was chosen to be the **Democratic candidate**. In November 2008, he was elected president.

Even though Hillary didn't become president, no other woman had come as close. Hillary's efforts made new opportunities possible for other women.

A New Dream

Barack became president in 2009. Before taking office, Barack asked Hillary to be the secretary of state.

Hillary made a special promise to serve as secretary of state.

Hillary was excited to begin her new job. The secretary of state is the head of the U.S. Department of State. Hillary meets with world leaders and advises the president.

Over the years, Hillary's work has helped many Americans. People are excited to see what's next for Hillary Rodham Clinton.

Hillary meets leaders of other countries.

Important Dates

1947 Hillary Rodham is born on October 26.

1969 Hillary graduates from Wellesley College.

1973 Hillary graduates from Yale Law School.

1975 Hillary marries Bill Clinton.

1980 Chelsea Clinton is born.

1993 Hillary becomes the First Lady when Bill becomes U.S. president.

2001 Hillary becomes a U.S. senator.

2006 Hillary is elected to the U.S. Senate a second time.

2007 Hillary announces she will run for U.S. president.

2009 Hillary becomes the U.S. secretary of state.

Important Words

candidate (KAN-duh-dayt) a person who seeks a political office.
Democratic relating to the Democratic political party. Democrats believe in social change and strong government.
graduation (gra-juh-WAY-shuhn) an event held to mark the completion of a level of schooling.
impeach to charge someone for doing wrong while serving in a public office.
lawyer (LAW-yuhr) a person who gives people advice on laws or represents them in court.
politics the art or science of government. A politician works in politics.
public service work done to build a community or support its members.
research careful study in order to learn facts about a subject.
rival one who competes for the same position as another.

Web Sites

To learn more about Hillary Rodham Clinton, visit ABDO Publishing Company online. Web sites about Hillary Rodham Clinton are featured on our Book Links page. These links are routinely monitored and updated to provide the most current information available.

www.abdopublishing.com

Index

Arkansas **12, 13**

Clinton, Bill **12, 13, 14, 15, 16, 17, 20, 22, 25, 30**

Clinton, Chelsea **14, 15, 16, 20, 25, 30**

Connecticut **9**

Democratic Party **9, 25, 26, 27**

Department of State, U.S. **29**

education **7, 8, 9, 10, 12, 30**

Illinois **6, 25**

It Takes a Village **19**

Living History **21**

Massachusetts **8, 10**

New York **22, 23**

Nixon, Richard **10, 11**

Obama, Barack **25, 26, 27, 28, 29**

Rodham, Dorothy **6, 7**

Rodham, Hugh (brother) **6, 7**

Rodham, Hugh (father) **6, 7**

Rodham, Tony **6, 7**

Rose Law Firm **13, 14**

Senate, U.S. **22, 30**

Washington, D.C. **16, 20**

White House **13, 16, 18, 21**

APR 11 2010
25-65